We Like the Summer

Katie Peters

GRL Consultants,
Diane Craig and Monica Marx,
Certified Literacy Specialists

Lerner Publications ◆ Minneapolis

Note from a GRL Consultant
This Pull Ahead leveled book has been carefully designed for beginning readers.
A team of guided reading literacy experts has reviewed and leveled the book to
ensure readers pull ahead and experience success.

Lerner Publications Company
A division of Lerner Publishing Group, Inc.
241 First Avenue North
Minneapolis, MN 55401 USA

For reading levels and more information, look up this title at www.lernerbooks.com.

Main body text set in Memphis Pro 24/39
Typeface provided by Linotype.

Photo Acknowledgments
The images in this book are used with the permission of: © Shutterstock, pp. 3, 4–5,
16 (bottom right); © iStockphoto, pp. 6–7, 8–9, 10–11, 12–13, 14–15, 16 (top left), 16
(top center), 16 (top right), 16 (bottom left)

Front cover: © Shutterstock

Library of Congress Cataloging-in-Publication Data

Names: Peters, Katie, author.
Title: We like the summer / Katie Peters.
Description: Minneapolis, MN : Lerner Publications, [2020] | Series: Seasons all
    around me (Pull ahead readers - Nonfiction) | Audience: Ages 4–7. | Audience:
    K to grade 3. | Includes index.
Identifiers: LCCN 2018058180 (print) | LCCN 2018060468 (ebook) | ISBN 9781541562370
    (eb pdf) | ISBN 9781541558717 (lb : alk. paper) | ISBN 9781541573468 (pb : alk. paper)
Subjects: LCSH: Summer—Juvenile literature. | Seasons—Juvenile literature.
Classification: LCC QB637.6 (ebook) | LCC QB637.6 .P475 2020 (print) | DDC 508.2—dc23

LC record available at https://lccn.loc.gov/2018058180

Manufactured in the United States of America
1 – CG – 7/15/19

Contents

We Like the Summer

We like the sun.

We like the grass.

We like the flowers.

We like the beach.

We like the pool.